CLASSIC GUITAR   Compiled & Edi

MEL BAY PRESENTS
COMPLETE
SOR STUDIES

David Grimes uses and endorses LaBella strings

2 3 4 5 6 7 8 9 0

© 1994 BY MEL BAY PUBLICATIONS, INC., PACIFIC, MO 63069.
ALL RIGHTS RESERVED. INTERNATIONAL COPYRIGHT SECURED. B.M.I. MADE AND PRINTED IN U.S.A.

MEL BAY®

Visit us on the Web at http://www.melbay.com — E-mail us at email@melbay.com

CONTENTS

INTRODUCTION

The studies of Fernando Sor have long been valued highly among the indispensable elements of a guitarist's training. A number of prominent virtuosi attribute a large portion of their development to the diligent study of these works.

Fernando Sor (1778-1839) was a leader of the "first generation" of guitarists who played instruments similar to the ones in use today (though smaller), and it is remarkable that he was able to penetrate so deeply into the technique of the instrument. Individual studies address an impressive array of technical and musical topics, including proper left-hand fingering, training of the right hand, interval and chord formations, scales, arpeggios, repeated notes, ligados, barring, natural harmonics, control of note duration, balance of melody versus accompaniment, and the handling of contrapuntal voices. A careful study of these pieces will lay the groundwork for a solid technique and allow the guitarist to build the control necessary for the expression of his or her musical concepts.

Andrés Segovia, in his venerable edition of twenty of the studies, remarked that, "Not many Masters have succeeded in their studies for the gradual development of the instrument's technique in achieving the right balance between the pedagogical purpose and the natural musical beauty." Sor's studies, so vital for technical and musical training, have a substance and beauty that suit them well for concert performance. Even in the simplest studies Sor was rarely content to limit himself to the formulaic repetition of an arpeggio or other figure. His beginning pieces show a serious and noble musical concept unusual in the guitar's student repertoire. This high musical quality makes these studies ideal vehicles for the development of such musical fundamentals as tone production, melodic shaping and phrasing.

Throughout his career, Sor's music was much in demand, and he was pressured by publishers and the public to compose easier music that less accomplished players could master. His first sets of studies, op. 6 and op. 29, are relatively advanced, with later publications offering studies more suitable for beginning and intermediate students. Each opus presents its studies in a more-or-less graded order, and there is considerable overlapping among the various sets, but the general progression would be from op. 60 and 44 (beginning to intermediate) to op. 35 and 31 (intermediate to advanced) to op. 6 and 29 (advanced). That is the ordering adopted for this edition.

In preparing this edition, I have worked from Sor's original publications, but I have incorporated some alterations that appear in those studies that Napoleon Coste chose to include in his *Methode complete pour la Guitarre par Ferdinand Sor.* I have also undeniably been influenced by Segovia's concepts of fingering, since his edition, *Twenty Studies for the Guitar by Fernando Sor,* was the standard during my own formative years. In a number of instances, I have corrected misprints (some obvious, some apparent), modernized the notation and rectified some inconsistencies. The fingerings are based upon Sor's own, but I have altered and extended the indications where I felt it was necessary or useful, either to clarify ideas or to make the studies more relevant to the contemporary player.

Some developments in technique since Sor's day have been incorporated in this edition. Sor's concept of technique involved using the stronger fingers wherever possible, even when that entailed excessive shifting, whereas most contemporary players stress the importance of developing all the fingers to their utmost capability and reducing the frequency of shifting. The difference shows up most clearly in the studies in intervals (op. 6, no. 6 is the best-known example).

Sor gave the right-hand thumb a very prominent role (often denoting its use consistently with down-stems), and the exclusive use of the thumb on a particular voice is still extremely useful in differentiating between voices. Several of Sor's studies are devoted primarily to the development of the thumb's agility. See, for example, op. 35, no. 17 and op. 29, no. 11, where the thumb is required to leap accurately from string to string.

Sor's smaller guitar allowed fingerings that entail formidable extensions on a modern guitar. See, for example, op. 35, no. 20 and op. 31, no. 16. In some cases alternate fingerings are available, but in others there is no way of avoiding some rather heroic stretches without sacrificing the musical intent.

Sor advised the student to maintain each left-hand finger on its fretted note until that finger is needed for another note, or until a lower note is needed on that string. The goals of this idea are to stabilize the hand, reduce the number of movements and sustain as much harmony as possible. The blanket rule, however, is much too general, since the factors of harmonic movement and phrasing must also be considered. The proper ending of a note is vitally important, and often overlooked.

Sor's insistence upon maintaining fingers in place extended to the systematic use of guide and pivot fingers. In some cases, this led to remarkably "modern" fingerings using "backward" formations. Examples are found in op. 60, no. 18 (line 7, measure 1) and in op. 31, no. 17 (line 5, measure 2).

I would recommend strongly that the student read David Tanenbaum's *The Essential Studies: Fernando Sor's 20 Estudios* (Guitar Solo Publications, 1991). This excellent series of essays not only provides helpful advice on the studies themselves, but serves as a superb example of the depth of study and attention to detail that these pieces deserve.

INTRODUCTION TO THE STUDY OF THE GUITAR
in Twenty-five Progressive Lessons

Fernando Sor
Opus 60

(Beginning-to-Intermediate Level)

No. 3

No. 4

No. 5

No. 6

Fine

No. 7

Fine

10

No. 10

No. 11

No. 12

No. 13

13

No. 14

Andante

No. 15

Allegro

No. 16

Andantino

Allegro moderato

No. 17

*This page has been
left blank to avoid
awkward page turns*

No. 18

Fine

No. 19

No. 20

No. 21

No. 22

Allegretto moderato

Andantino

No. 23

23

No. 24

Allegro moderato

Fine

24

Tune 6th string to D

No. 25

"For the harmonic sounds, the lower notes indicate the manner of playing, and the upper notes show the result produced. The 3 with the overline (/3) indicates that the sound should be produced a little above the third fret, since there is no node directly over it, and below it one produces another a minor third higher." (Sor) These are all "natural harmonics" produced by plucking with the right hand while the left hand touches the open strings at the frets specified (down-stems). The smaller notes above (up-stems) indicate the resultant notes.

*This page has been
left blank to avoid
awkward page turns*

TWENTY-FOUR LITTLE PROGRESSIVE PIECES
to Serve as Lessons

Fernando Sor
Opus 44

(Beginning-to-Intermediate Level)

No. 3 Andantino

No. 4 — Allegretto moderato

No. 5 — Andantino

No. 6

Moderato

No. 9 — Andantino

No. 10 **Allegretto**

No. 11 **Andante**

No. 12

Andantino

Fine

No. 15

No 16

No.17

No. 18 Marche

No. 19

No. 20

No. 23 **Allegro moderato**

Fine

No. 24
Valse

TWENTY-FOUR EASY EXERCISES

Fernando Sor
Opus 35

(Intermediate-to-Advanced Level)

No. 1

No. 2

No. 3

Larghetto

No. 4

This page has been left blank to avoid awkward page turns

No. 5

No. 6

No. 7

No. 8

54

No. 10

57

No. 11

Allegretto

Tune 6th string to F

Andantino moderato

No. 12

No. 14   **Andante**

No. 15   **Allegretto.**

CII

No. 16

Moderato

No. 17

64

No. 18

Andantino

No. 19

This page has been
left blank to avoid
awkward page turns

No. 20

Tempo di minuetto

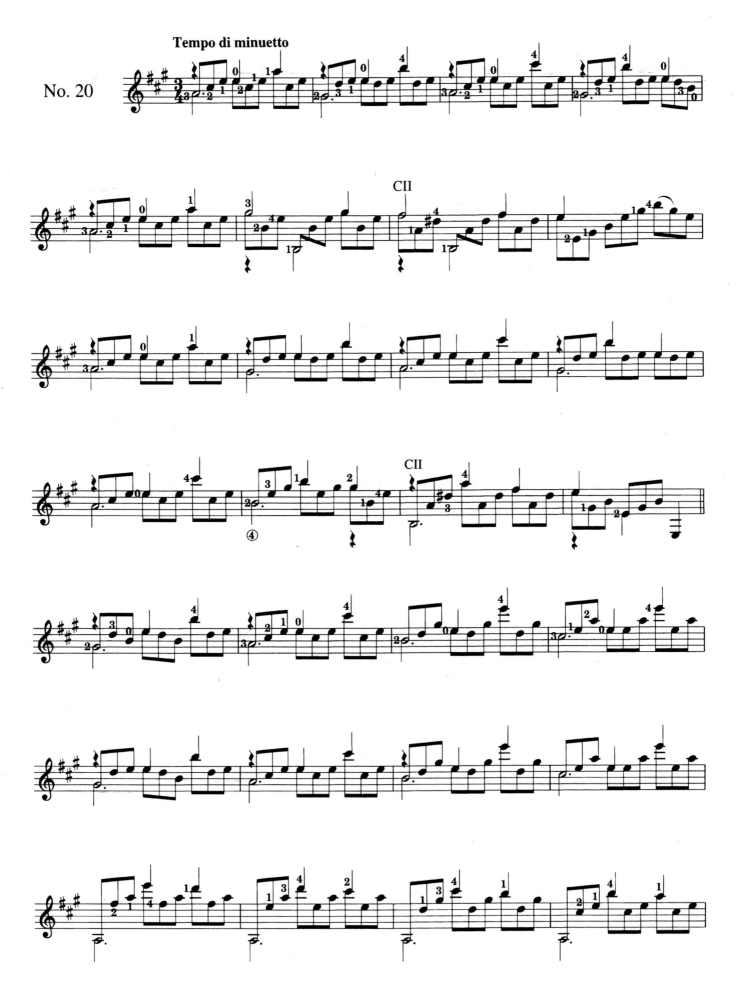

No. 21

No. 22

Allegretto

No. 23

No. 24

Allegro moderato

73

This page has been
left blank to avoid
awkward page turns

TWENTY-FOUR PROGRESSIVE LESSONS

Fernando Sor
Opus 31

(Intermediate-to-Advanced Level)

LEÇON I

Andante

LEÇON II

Andante

Fine

Allegretto moderato

LEÇON
III

LEÇON
IV

LEÇON
V

LEÇON
VI

LEÇON VIII

84

LEÇON
X

Cantabile

LEÇON
XI

Tune 6th string to D

Andante

LEÇON
XII

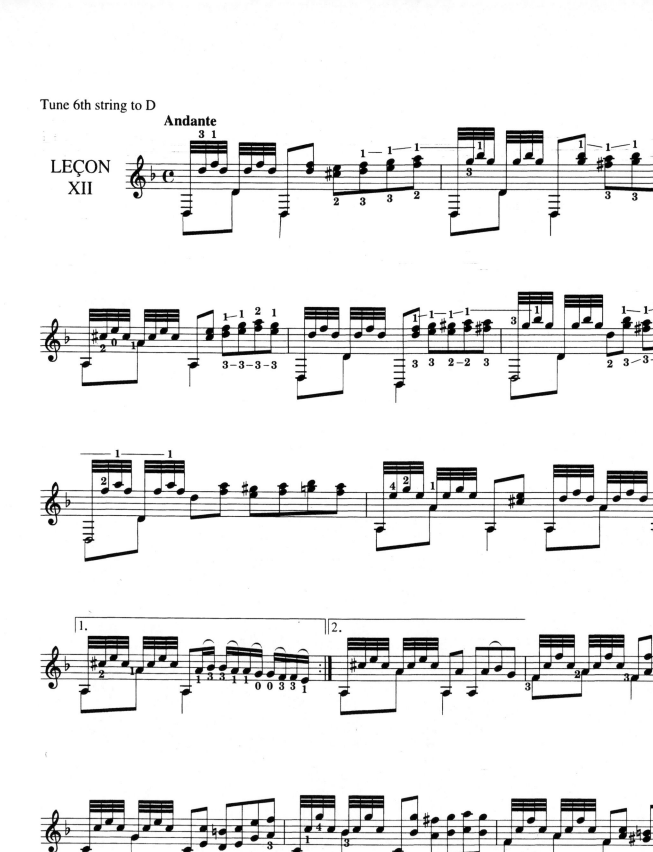

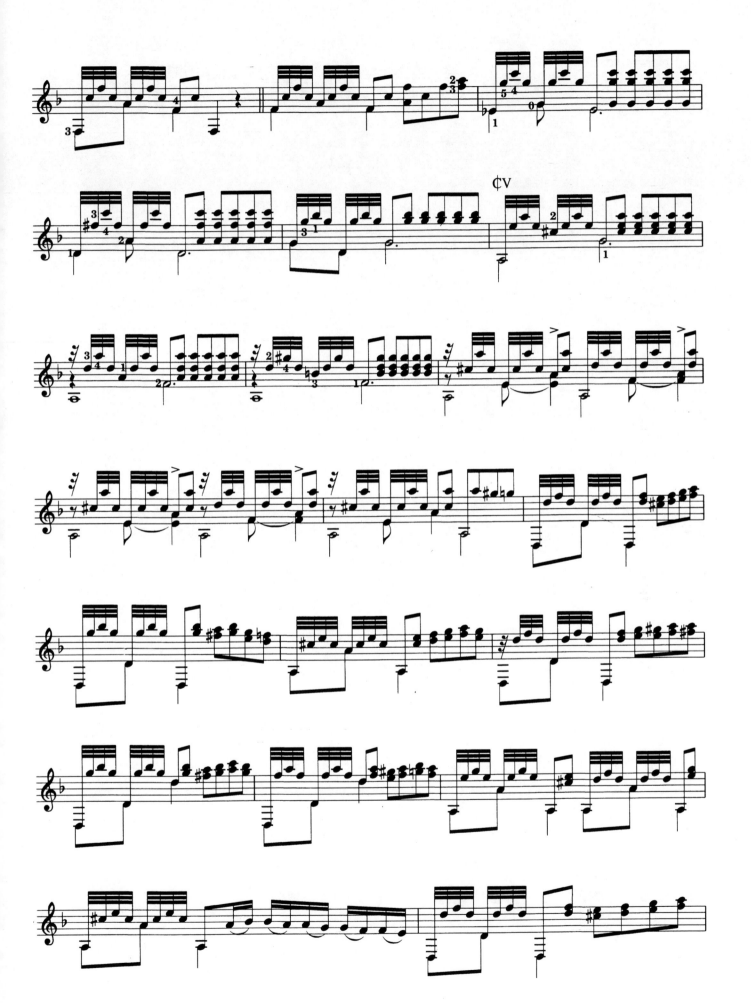

CI

ĊIII

LEÇON XIV

Andantino

*This page has been
left blank to avoid
awkward page turns*

LEÇON
XV

LEÇON
XVI

Moderato

LEÇON
XVIII

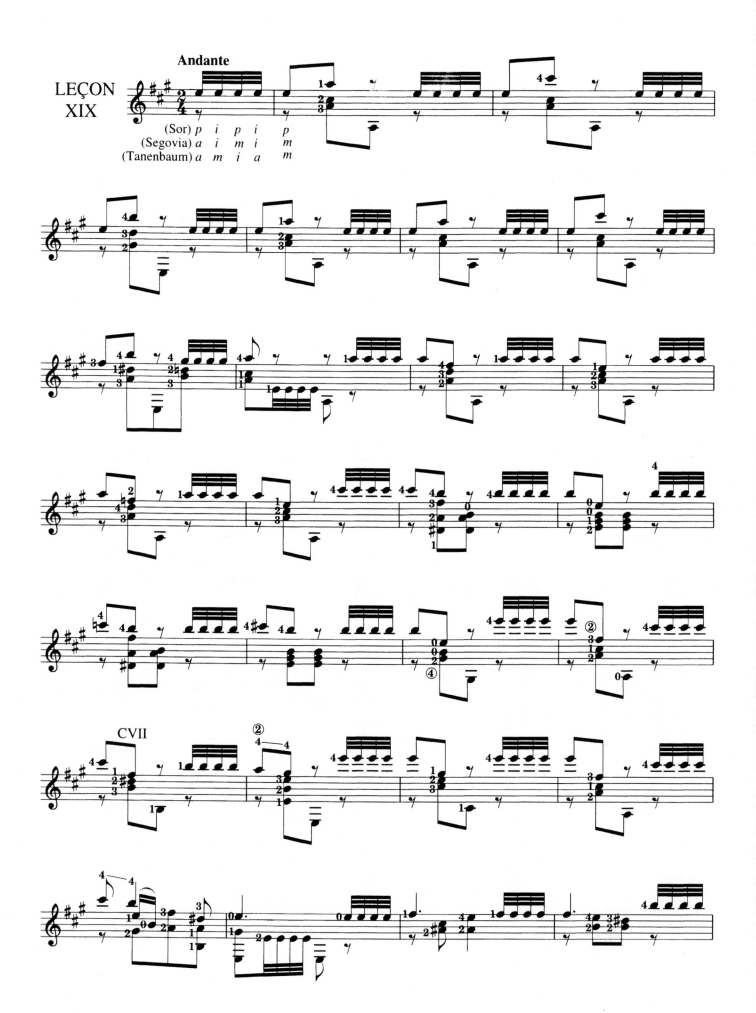

LEÇON
XIX

(Sor) *p i p i p*
(Segovia) *a i m i m*
(Tanenbaum) *a m i a m*

CVII

LEÇON
XX

Andante allegro

100

LEÇON XXI

Andantino cantabile

Mouvement de prière religieuse

LEÇON
XXIII

103

LEÇON
XXIV

Allegretto moderato

*This page has been
left blank to avoid
awkward page turns*

STUDIES FOR THE GUITAR

Fernando Sor
Opus 6

(Advanced Level)

STUDIO
1

Allegro moderato

108

Andante allegro

STUDIO
2

STUDIO
3

STUDIO
4

Allegretto

STUDIO
5

STUDIO
6

Allegro

Tune 6th String to D

Allegro

STUDIO
7

CII

STUDIO
8

Andantino

119

Tune 6th String to D

STUDIO
9

121

STUDIO
10

Moderato

123

STUDIO
11

Allegro moderato

STUDIO
12

*This page has been
left blank to avoid
awkward page turns*

TWELVE STUDIES FOR THE GUITAR
to Serve as a Continuation of the First Twelve (Opus 6)

Fernando Sor
Opus 29

(Advanced Level)

STUDIO
13

132

STUDIO
14

Andante moderato

CIII

135

137

STUDIO
15

138

STUDIO
16

Lento assai

STUDIO 17

Allegro moderato

This page has been
left blank to avoid
awkward page turns

Andante

STUDIO
18

146

STUDIO
19

148

This page has been
left blank to avoid
awkward page turns

Tune 6th String To D

STUDIO 20

Moderato

This study is entirely in natural harmonics. The numbers indicate the frets at which the sounds will be produced.

Tune 6th String To D

The result of the harmonics will sound thus.

This page has been
left blank to avoid
awkward page turns

STUDIO
22

STUDIO
23

STUDIO
24